Samuel French Acting Edition

The Poorly-Written Play Festival

Just Possibly the Worst One-Act Play Ever Written

by Carolyn Gage

SAMUELFRENCH.COM   SAMUELFRENCH.CO.UK

Copyright © 2016 by Carolyn Gage
All Rights Reserved

THE POORLY-WRITTEN PLAY FESTIVAL is fully protected under the copyright laws of the United States of America, the British Commonwealth, including Canada, and all other countries of the Copyright Union. All rights, including professional and amateur stage productions, recitation, lecturing, public reading, motion picture, radio broadcasting, television and the rights of translation into foreign languages are strictly reserved.

ISBN 978-0-573-70578-6

www.SamuelFrench.com
www.SamuelFrench.co.uk

FOR PRODUCTION ENQUIRIES

UNITED STATES AND CANADA
Info@SamuelFrench.com
1-866-598-8449

UNITED KINGDOM AND EUROPE
Plays@SamuelFrench.co.uk
020-7255-4302

Each title is subject to availability from Samuel French, depending upon country of performance. Please be aware that *THE POORLY-WRITTEN PLAY FESTIVAL* may not be licensed by Samuel French in your territory. Professional and amateur producers should contact the nearest Samuel French office or licensing partner to verify availability.

CAUTION: Professional and amateur producers are hereby warned that *THE POORLY-WRITTEN PLAY FESTIVAL* is subject to a licensing fee. Publication of this play(s) does not imply availability for performance. Both amateurs and professionals considering a production are strongly advised to apply to Samuel French before starting rehearsals, advertising, or booking a theatre. A licensing fee must be paid whether the title(s) is presented for charity or gain and whether or not admission is charged. Professional/Stock licensing fees are quoted upon application to Samuel French.

No one shall make any changes in this title(s) for the purpose of production. No part of this book may be reproduced, stored in a retrieval system, or transmitted in any form, by any means, now known or yet to be invented, including mechanical, electronic, photocopying, recording, videotaping, or otherwise, without the prior written permission of the publisher. No one shall upload this title(s), or part of this title(s), to any social media websites.

For all enquiries regarding motion picture, television, and other media rights, please contact Samuel French.

MUSIC USE NOTE

Licensees are solely responsible for obtaining formal written permission from copyright owners to use copyrighted music in the performance of this play and are strongly cautioned to do so. If no such permission is obtained by the licensee, then the licensee must use only original music that the licensee owns and controls. Licensees are solely responsible and liable for all music clearances and shall indemnify the copyright owners of the play(s) and their licensing agent, Samuel French, against any costs, expenses, losses and liabilities arising from the use of music by licensees. Please contact the appropriate music licensing authority in your territory for the rights to any incidental music.

IMPORTANT BILLING AND CREDIT REQUIREMENTS

If you have obtained performance rights to this title, please refer to your licensing agreement for important billing and credit requirements.

THE POORLY-WRITTEN PLAY FESTIVAL was first produced at the Fourth Annual Maine Short Play Festival by Michael Levine and Acorn Productions, at the St. Lawrence Arts Center in Portland, Maine on April 1, 2005. The performance was directed by Tavia Gilbert. The stage manager was Liz McMahon. The cast was as follows:

LOMAN . . . . Allen Bergeron
EUGENE . . . . Jeremiah McDonald
HEDDA . . . . Heather Thomson
MRS. BRACKNELL . . . . Muriel Kenderdine
STELLA . . . . Tamara Kissane
STRANGER . . . . Seth Berner

CHARACTERS

LOMAN – The artistic director, a stick-in-the-mud.
EUGENE – The technical director, a queen.
HEDDA – The literary manager, a bitch.
MRS. BRACKNELL – The wealthy benefactress, a crashing bore.
STELLA – The costumer, a tart.
STRANGER – A man with a mustache.

SETTING

The Green Room of a community theatre.

TIME

The present.

(Lights come up on the interior of the green room of a small amateur theater. There is a large table center stage, around which are seated **LOMAN, HEDDA, STELLA, EUGENE, MRS. BRACKNELL,** *and a* **STRANGER.** *There is a large pile of scripts in front of each character, except the* **STRANGER,** *who has a single manuscript in front of him.* **LOMAN** *is addressing the others.)*

LOMAN. *(Clearing his throat.)* Well… I see that all of us readers for the Festival of Poorly-Written Plays are here today. And I see that we have each brought with us the pile of submissions that I – Loman Dexterhaven – as the beleaguered, but indefatigable artistic director of this admittedly deserving, but habitually impecunious theatre company, have assigned you all to read. I assume that we have all read them and that we have all come here today prepared to make our recommendation for which of these plays to include in this, our first annual Festival of Poorly-Written Plays. Furthermore, I assume that we have educated ourselves on the finer points of the poorly-written play, in order to select specimens that go beyond such obvious defects as blatant exposition, contrived names for the characters, and lack of conflict. *(Complete agreement all around.)* Good. Well, then, why don't we go around the table, introduce ourselves, and say a little bit about who we are, which plays we have selected and why… Hedda, since you're our literary manager, why don't you start?

HEDDA. Well, Loman, why should we introduce ourselves? We've all known each other for years, except for that complete stranger seated at the end of the table. Nobody has the faintest idea what he's doing here.

LOMAN. Good point, Hedda. So are we all in agreement *not* to go around the table and introduce ourselves, then? *(Complete agreement.)* Hedda, did you have a recommendation?

HEDDA. Well, Loman, I hate it when the action is completely unmotivated – or, worse, when it's actually counter-indicated by something that has just taken place. *(Complete agreement.)*

MRS. BRACKNELL. *(Brightly.)* Well, since we're all going around the table introducing ourselves and telling why we're here, I guess it's my turn...

HEDDA. *(Graciously.)* Please...

MRS. BRACKNELL. I'm Mrs. Bracknell, and, as a serious patron of the arts and as the primary benefactor of this company, I feel a certain personal responsibility for banishing the ignorance that accounts for the growing number of poorly-written plays we must all suffer in the theatre today. This festival is a humorous way to raise awareness as to what constitutes a poorly-written play, thereby – one might hope – elevating the standard for both playwrights and audiences. The Festival of Poorly-Written Plays was my idea, and I am so committed to the project, that I have made my subsidy of the rest of the season contingent on its production.

LOMAN. *(An aside to the audience.)* Which is the only reason why I agreed to this asinine plan...

MRS. BRACKNELL. It has been gratifying to see the company's enthusiastic response –

EUGENE, STELLA, HEDDA. *(Collective aside.)* Not.

MRS. BRACKNELL. The Festival is being dedicated to the memory of my late husband, Bramford Bracknell, who disappeared a year ago during an elk-hunting trip in Colorado. Bramford, rest his soul, loved the theatre. I don't think he ever saw a play that he didn't like. No matter how many times he was subjected to sentimental and fatuous speeches by characters purporting to be comedic, but who, in actuality, were nothing more than tedious bores, he would sit there, bless his heart, applauding like a trained seal. Poor Bramford. *(An* *aside.)* He wouldn't have known a good play if it bit him on the ass. *(To the others.)* But I never complained. I accompanied him faithfully to every appalling amateur, new-play festival, every interminable evening of insipid one-acts, every solo show by some member of an oppressed minority – he insisted that we see them all! And I never said no. You see, I was his second wife. His first wife ran off with a second cousin, who was actually my step-brother, making me, technically, Bramford's step-sister-in-law. By a remarkable coincidence, my *own* first husband turned out to have been *his* dentist! But what is even more astounding is that my dentist turns out to have been *his* adopted daughter – not the dentist's, but my second husband's…with his first wife, of course…

LOMAN. Mrs. Bracknell…

MRS. BRACKNELL. Yes?

LOMAN. Do you have a play that you would like to recommend?

MRS. BRACKNELL. Yes, I do. Here… *(She pulls a script from her pile.)* Terrible thing… Take it! The relationship histories were so complicated it was impossible to keep them straight… And, then, all this useless information about a character about whom we have no interest at all, who never even appears…

LOMAN. Excellent, Mrs. Bracknell. And now, Eugene…?

EUGENE. Is it my turn?

LOMAN. We were going around the table.

EUGENE. Well, I am concerned that a poorly-written play…

LOMAN. Your name?

EUGENE. Oh… Eugene. I'm the technical director. Now, I've lost what I was trying to say…

HEDDA. *(Prompting.)* "I'm concerned that a poorly-written play…"

EUGENE. It's *my* turn!

HEDDA. I was just repeating what you said!

EUGENE. Now, I'm totally confused.

LOMAN. It's all right, Eugene. Just take your time.

EUGENE. Well, I hate those scenes where characters mindlessly snipe at each other as a substitute for real dialogue. You don't see Hamlet doing that.

HEDDA. Domestic drama! Why don't you just admit it? You don't like domestic drama. And that's because you don't like to build middle-class living rooms. Why not just come out and say it and stop pretending that it's because the plays are badly written.

EUGENE. Why don't you stop putting words in my mouth? I can speak for myself. Who wants to listen to people bicker like dysfunctional families?

HEDDA. That would be Albee, Miller, Shepard, Williams, O'Neill…

EUGENE. *(To **LOMAN**.)* I thought you said it was my turn?

LOMAN. Hedda…

HEDDA. Well, really, Loman, he should just say what he means.

LOMAN. Well, Hedda, let's give him the chance to.

EUGENE. *My concern is* that a poorly-written play will have set requirements that strain the resources of the stage… like a tornado, or a flood, or an elephant stampede. *My concern is* that the literary manager and the artistic director are always picking out plays with no thought for the technical director and a technical director's budget.

LOMAN. Eugene…

EUGENE. Let me finish! When I was a child, I would come home from school…at least I would come home on the days when I had been *allowed* to go to school, and there would be my mother, in a stained and threadbare slip, slumped over the kitchen table, her eyes staring vacantly past the half-crushed cigarette still burning in the ashtray next to a row of empty beer bottles standing like impotent sentinels between her and the memories that tormented her – **(LOMAN** *starts to interrupt, but*

EUGENE *freezes him with a look.)* She was waiting for me…waiting for the iceman…waiting for Godot… *(***HEDDA** *yawns audibly.)* And she would hand me a list of things she wanted me to buy at the store. I can still see those words today – scrawled like hieroglyphics in that shaky handwriting of hers – words forever etched with the acid of remorse on the tablets of my memory: Alka-Seltzer… Spam… Little Debbies…*but – (He pauses painfully.)* She would never give me enough money to buy everything on the list. So it would be up to me – up to poor, little, ten-year-old Eugene – to figure out which items she could actually afford and which ones she could do without, but no matter how carefully I calculated or how hard I tried to get it right, the result was always the same: I had chosen the wrong things. If I had brought home the Alka-Seltzer, but not the Spam… then it would be the Spam she had her heart set on, but if it had been the Spam I had brought home in place of the Little Debbies, well, you can guess… *(Nodding solemnly.)* The Little Debbies. It would be the Little Debbies she could not live without. *(Turning savagely on his colleagues.)* And *that's* what it's like working for all of you!

STELLA. *(Studying her nails.)* I don't even *like* Little Debbies.

EUGENE. The set! It's the set! You describe it, you explain it, you sketch it, but then you never give me the budget to build it the way you want – so I have to decide where to cut corners, *but no matter what I decide, I'm always wrong! Always wrong!*

STELLA. *(Interrupting his tirade.)* Oh, God, Eugene… Pinch it off!

EUGENE. You see? You see?

> *(Just then a cell phone rings and all the characters, except the* **STRANGER**, *dig for their phones. It's* **STELLA***'s phone, and she improvises obscure dialogue over the next few lines.)*

LOMAN. *(Appeasing* **EUGENE**.*)* All right, all right…

HEDDA. So far nobody has said anything about the "talking heads" play where everyone just sits around a table talking, all dialogue and no action? How about that?

STELLA. *(Hanging up abruptly, she turns to* **HEDDA.***)* You've written a play, haven't you?

HEDDA. *(Shocked.)* How did you know that?

STELLA. Just a guess… *(Aside to the audience.)* I know she's written a play, because I've stolen it. It's called *The Rat Takes the Cheese*, and I covered up her name and put it in Loman's pile of poorly-written plays. I can't wait to see her face when he names it as a candidate for the festival, which, of course, he will, because it's terrible.

HEDDA. *(Aside.)* How could she have known about my play? It is my most carefully-guarded secret! I am just biding my time in this two-bit, literary manager position, until I can make the right connections to launch my play. It's the best thing that's been written for the American stage in two hundred years. I have poured my life blood into it –

STELLA. Well, I'm Stella, and I'm the costumer for the company –

HEDDA. *(Cutting her off.)* You interrupted my aside!

STELLA. How could I have done that? *(Aside.)* Doesn't she know the other characters can't hear an aside?

HEDDA. What? *(Aside.)* Did she say something to you?

STELLA. What? *(Aside.)* Don't listen to her!

HEDDA. What? *(Aside.)* Bitch!

STELLA. What?

HEDDA. What?

STELLA. As I was saying… *(Aside.)* …before I was so rudely interrupted…

> *(***HEDDA** *starts to say something, but* **STELLA** *glares at her, and resumes speaking to the group.)*

I am the costumer, and, although there are those who think that my area of expertise should be limited to the picking out of patterns and fabrics, I am, in fact, an excellent judge of plays. You see, the person who has no actual hands-on experience with production, whose only experience is with literary criticism and pet theories of out-of-touch professors hoping to carve out some little niche for themselves in academia –

LOMAN. *(Bellowing, Stanley-Kowalski-style.)* Stel-la-a-a-ah! *(She turns.)* Have you chosen a play?

STELLA. Yes, I have. And so far, all I've heard has been… *(To* **EUGENE.***)* Talk about impractical sets…

(To **HEDDA.***)*

Too much dialogue…

(To **MRS. BRACKNELL.***)*

And plots that are hard to follow…

(To **LOMAN.***)*

but I think you're overlooking the most fatal mistake a playwright can make…

HEDDA. *(Nasty.)* Which is?

STELLA. *(To* **HEDDA.***)* Which is an utterly repellant central character!

HEDDA. This is about me, isn't it, Stella? Why don't you just come out and say it? You're jealous of me. You've always been jealous of me.

(Suddenly the **STRANGER** *rises and crosses toward the door. As he passes* **HEDDA**, *she slips him a folded piece of paper. He exits.)*

LOMAN. Well, all right, then… I guess it's my turn…

(A phone rings again. Same business with cell phones. This time the call is for **EUGENE**. *He improvises obscure dialogue over* **LOMAN***'s lines.)*

Well, there are a lot of things I don't like in a play. For example, I don't like…

(Raising his voice to drown out **EUGENE.***)*

...gimmicks! Especially when it's something that wasn't funny the first time, but then the playwright has it happen again and again, as if it's somehow going to acquire humor by repetition.

*(***EUGENE*** hangs up.)*

But, bad plays...? I mean, there are so many things...worthless secrets, implausible coincidences, foreshadowing that's so heavy-handed, the playwright might as well beat you over the head with it. If it's all so predictable, why not go home at intermission? *(Aside to the audience.)* Frankly, that's what I think our audiences are going to do at this festival. There's so much bad theatre produced anyway, who needs a special festival for it? You know, Mrs. Bracknell has actually left us a huge endowment in her will. If she would just drop dead, we could have her money without all this butt-kissing... *(The* **STRANGER** *re-enters.)*

EUGENE. *(Bursting out.)* Okay, you know what I can't stand? I can't stand death! *(***HEDDA*** rolls her eyes.)* I can't stand it when a play ends in death. And I'm not talking about *Hamlet* or *Othello* or something. I'm talking about your average Joe Schmoe, and the playwright can't think of any better way to wrap things up than to have some phony-baloney death scene at the end of the play. Doesn't work. You can't kill just anybody and expect it to be a tragedy. *(A long pause.)*

HEDDA. So, Loman, did you want to recommend one of the plays from your pile?

LOMAN. Well, Hedda, they were all terrible, but there *was* one that was especially stinko.

STELLA. *(Aside to the audience.)* Here it comes!

LOMAN. This playwright seemed not just under-endowed in terms of her ability to dramatize, but positively hell-bent on sabotaging whatever meager dramatic possibilities were inherent in her situations. The audience's expectations of a dramatically charged encounter would be awakened, only to be completely disappointed when the climactic scene failed to materialize.

STELLA. *(With glee.)* And what play was that, Loman?

LOMAN. Well, Stella...it is... *(He pulls a thick manuscript out of the pile.)* The Rat Takes the Cheese.

>*(Nobody says anything.* **EUGENE** *yawns.)*

STELLA. Hedda, don't you recognize the title of your own play? I stole it from your office and put it in with Loman's scripts, and now he's saying it's the worst play of all!

HEDDA. *(Genuinely puzzled.)* What's your point, Stella?

STELLA. You are a terrible writer! Your script is the worst one out of a whole stack of poorly-written plays! You set up a dramatic situation and then fail to provide the obligatory scene!

HEDDA. Oh... *(A long pause.* **HEDDA** *sighs and speaks with complete resignation.)* Well, I'm disappointed, of course. Who wouldn't be? But not everyone who writes a play can be a playwright.

LOMAN. Stella, I believe you forgot to tell us which play you selected...

STELLA. Me? Well, obviously Hedda's – but in terms of my own stack? I chose one where the characters suddenly reverse their positions for no reason at all. *(She pulls out one of the scripts.)* But, maybe that's not a strong enough reason. I don't know... *(Sincerely deferring to* **HEDDA**.*)* I'm just the costumer. Really, we should ask Hedda. I mean, she's the expert on picking plays. I think a background in literary criticism is absolutely essential for –

STRANGER. *(Rising.)* Stella, I can't take this much longer...

STELLA. Who are you?

STRANGER. Don't you know, Stella?

STELLA. No... Stranger.

STRANGER. Well, Stella, you should...

STELLA. Why should I?

STRANGER. Because, Stella, we used to –

STELLA. Oh, my God! Not the –

STRANGER. Yes, and not just the –

STELLA. You're right! And there was the –

STRANGER. Exactly. So now you see –

STELLA. Yes, yes… *(He nods.)* But, my God! It's been fifteen years! I had forgotten…

STRANGER. But, Stella, as you see, I have not. *(He begins to write feverishly in his manuscript.)*

MRS. BRACKNELL. And who is this obnoxious stranger? I thought we all agreed we would go around the table and introduce ourselves… I don't remember any member of this theatre company with a mustache!

LOMAN. You're right. *(To the STRANGER.)* Who are you?

STRANGER. *(Looking up from his writing.)* Don't you know?

LOMAN. Would I have asked?

STRANGER. Clever, but not clever enough –

LOMAN. Is that for you to say, or for me to find out?

HEDDA. Stop it! Stop this childish charade! Shall I tell you all who this is?

EUGENE. *(Suddenly roused.)* No! *(They turn and look at him.)* Ah-ha! You didn't expect me to say anything, did you? Yes, the little mouse can roar! *(He roars.)* Good old Eugene… Good, old, no-trouble-at-all Eugene… Good, old Eugene who's always so nice about staying late and opening early. Good, old Eugene who's always behind the scenes, but never in the spotlight… Well, let me tell you, there's a lot that goes on behind the curtain that the rest of you will never know anything about…

(He crosses to the STRANGER and rips off his mustache. Collective gasps.)

MRS. BRACKNELL. My husband!

LOMAN. So you didn't die on the hunting trip to Colorado after all!

STRANGER. *(Triumphantly.)* No, I didn't. *(An aside.)* In fact, I've never been to Colorado!

ALL. *(Collective aside.)* No!

STRANGER. *(To his wife.)* All those years that we subscribed to season after season of amateur theatre, all those years we attended new play festivals, and you thought I was enjoying it, didn't you? You thought I was enjoying those ridiculous plays with mysterious strangers, absurd disguises that wouldn't fool a three-year-old, missing-presumed-dead family members turning up again after years of absence... Well, I hated them! I hated every wretched minute of every boring, badly-written, miserably-directed, abominably-acted play I ever sat through – from the vantage point of those relentlessly uncomfortable chairs in those inevitably overheated or underheated, never-intended-for-performance spaces! I hated them, do you hear? I hated them!

MRS. BRACKNELL. Oh, Bramford, then, why, oh *why*, did you put us both through such misery *insisting* that we go?

STRANGER. Because I was *studying* them!

LOMAN. You were studying bad plays?

STRANGER. Yes, because I know it takes a real genius to write a good play – and I knew that I was not that gifted...*but* I did believe it would be possible, if I studied enough bad theatre, to incorporate every aspect of the poorly-written play, stretching the limits of taste and the bounds of banality, into a single dramatic – or, rather, non-dramatic – entity, thereby creating something so intentional in its mediocrity that it actually transcended the categories of "good play" and "bad play" – a piece of theatre that would stand in a class all its own, above – and also beneath – serious critical attention.

STELLA. *(Breathless.)* And, Bramford, have you written such a play?

STRANGER. I have, Stella, and it was not until just a few minutes ago, seeing you here, that I was able to put the final touch on my manuscript...

STELLA. And what *was* that final touch, Bramford?

STRANGER. A baffling reference to a scene that existed in an earlier draft of the play, but which has been completely eliminated from the current one.

STELLA. *(In awe.)* Yes.

MRS. BRACKNELL. But, Bramford, I don't understand… How could you possibly have known that I would propose and then fund a Festival of Poorly-Written Plays?

STRANGER. Ahh… That is easy enough to explain. You see, my dear, I know you better than you know yourself.

EUGENE. Wait! That may be all well-and-good as far as implausible explanations go, but what about the significant action that takes place offstage? Does your play have that? It can't be the worst play in the world unless the most interesting scene in the play takes place out of view of the audience.

STRANGER. Here… Here's the play.

(Tossing a thick manuscript at **EUGENE.***)*

Read it and see for yourself if it's in there.

*(***EUGENE** *takes the play and begins to read.)*

LOMAN. Wait a minute! You're not dead after all! That means that Mrs. Bracknell's will, which presumes you dead, is nullified. *(Aside to the audience.)* We will lose the endowment…unless…

STRANGER. *(Aside to the audience.)* …unless I die.

*(***LOMAN** *turns and stares at him. The* **STRANGER** *turns to him.)*

Isn't that what you were thinking?

LOMAN. Yes, but… *(Aside.)* How could he know what I was thinking…unless –

STRANGER. *(Aside.)* …Unless I could hear his aside?

*(***LOMAN** *turns and stares at the* **STRANGER.***)*

LOMAN. But… *(A fast aside.)* Do you think –

STRANGER. *(Finishing the thought in an even faster aside.)* ...I can hear his aside?

> *(Both men turn and stare at each other. Showdown.)*

EUGENE. *(Handing back the script.)* Yes, good... It's in there...

HEDDA. You read the entire play just now?

EUGENE. Yes, and the playwright has indeed placed the most significant action offstage. *(To the* **STRANGER.***)* Congratulations. And, I might add, it was gratifying to see that you have not overlooked the absurd compression of time in which a character takes only a few minutes to perform a task that, in real life, would easily take hours to accomplish.

STRANGER. Thank you. And now, am I correct in assuming that my play will be the highlight of your first annual Festival of Poorly-Written Plays?

HEDDA. *(Rising in high dudgeon.)* No, you are not correct! This is what is destroying the vitality of the modern theatre, this kind of nepotism! Your wife has funded this festival, and now you expect – even demand! – that we select your play for production! What about these other poor playwrights? *(She indicates the pile.)* What about these toilers in obscurity? Working-class playwrights, playwrights of color, lesbian and gay playwrights, *feminist* playwrights? Each one of these scripts has a story to tell, aside from the obvious narrative between the pages. Each one of these tells a tale of oppression, of desperate hope... Listen hard and you can hear them all whispering, "I have a dream..." How many of these playwrights had to forgo some small luxury, or even a necessity, in order to be able to afford to photocopy and mail these scripts? How many of them had to type out their manuscripts at computers at the public library? How many of them had to copy them at the office, after-hours, in order to save a few pennies? But, because your wife has paid for this festival, you think you can just waltz in here and place your script at the top of the pile, ahead of all these other playwrights who have been waiting so patiently, some of them for decades, to have their say and, hopefully, someday, to join the roster of dramatists recognized for having written plays worse than most. What makes your misogyny, your racism, your homophobia, your ageism, your ableism, your anti-Semitism, your fat phobia so different from theirs? What is it, except your classism, that would qualify you for preferential treatment? Does your play, for instance, have some exceptionally irrelevant break-out speech that is utterly inconsistent with the character who delivers it, serving no other function than to provide a soapbox for the political opinions of the playwright?

STRANGER. I would be more than happy to answer that, after I've gone to the bathroom. *(He exits.)*

LOMAN. *(To* **HEDDA.***)* I don't know what to do. Eugene, is the play really that bad?

EUGENE. Execrable.

HEDDA. It doesn't matter. It could be the worst play in the world, but if we produce it, everyone will say that the only reason we thought it was terrible is because of his wife's connection to the festival.

MRS. BRACKNELL. I think Bramford should know that you are talking about him behind his back. I'm going to get him.

(She exits. A cell phone rings.)

STELLA. Don't anybody get that!

(It rings again and then stops. Two shots are heard. **EUGENE** *runs out. The others wait awkwardly until he returns.)*

EUGENE. *(Running back in.)* Oh, my God... They're dead!

LOMAN. Who's dead?

EUGENE. Mrs. Bracknell and her husband, Bramford.

STELLA. How did it happen?

EUGENE. From the position of the bodies and the location of the powder marks, I think I am safe in saying that Mrs. Bracknell, confronting her husband on his abandonment of her, shot him, but he lived just long enough to wrest the gun from her hand and fire it at her.

HEDDA. Or, Bramford, obviously unstable from an accident he suffered while hunting elk in Colorado, was attempting to kill himself in the men's room, when Mrs. Bracknell rushed in and, in the attempt to wrest the gun from his hand, killed him unintentionally, and then, not able to face the prospects of yet another separation from her beloved husband with whom she had just reunited, she shot herself.

STELLA. *(Turning ferociously on* **HEDDA.***)* Or, maybe, it has something to do with a *note* that was slipped to Bramford earlier... A note perhaps about a tryst, say, in a men's room? What about that... "Hedda"? Or is that your real name?

HEDDA. I don't know what you're talking about!

STELLA. Oh, don't you?

HEDDA. *(Breaking down and weeping.)* Yes, yes... I gave him a note. I didn't think anyone would see.

LOMAN. Hedda, this is important...

HEDDA. And my name is not "Hedda!" It's "Ophelia."

LOMAN. Ophelia, this is important... What did the note say?

HEDDA. It said, "Your mustache is slipping."

EUGENE. Well, I think we should bring the bodies in. Their location together in the men's room will give rise to unfortunate speculation that could effectively hijack the narrative... *(He opens the door. Smoke pours in.)* Oh, my God! The building is in flames!

HEDDA. Bramford must have set a roll of toilet paper on fire before he killed himself!

EUGENE. Or, between the time he shot his wife and then died from his own wounds...

STELLA. *(Turning viciously toward* **HEDDA**.*)* Or, maybe, it was the *note* he set on fire!

HEDDA. No! No! I can't accept that responsibility! Bramford dead, and all because of some note about his mustache, which was slipping…? And it *was*! You all know it was! Why doesn't anyone say anything! Do you all hate me so much? I don't care… I don't care… I shall go mad! Do you hear? I shall go mad! La la la la la la…

LOMAN. *(Shaking* **HEDDA**.*)* This is no time for bad acting! Any minute now this very room will be engulfed in flames, which, if this were not a play… *(Aside.)* and it is – *(To* **HEDDA**.*)* …would mean that the entire theatre would burn to the ground, killing not only the actors, but also the members of the audience!

EUGENE. For which, of course, there is no contingency in the set budget…

LOMAN. I'm afraid there's only one thing left to do!

HEDDA. You're right…!

(She turns to **STELLA**, *who rises to the challenge.)*

STELLA. Gratuitous female nudity!

(Both women engage in frantic efforts to unfasten their clothing.)

LOMAN. No, stop it! That's not it!

(The women freeze.)

The only thing that can save us now is to wake up!

(All except **LOMAN** *immediately pretend to sleep.* **LOMAN** *looks at them for a moment.)*

No!

(They all wake up and look at him.)

We can't all be having the same dream! That won't work!

EUGENE. *(Suspicious, to* **LOMAN**.*)* What are you saying?

HEDDA. He's saying only *one* of us can be asleep.

STELLA. Which means the rest of will have only been a dream!

EUGENE. *(More suspicious, to* **STELLA.***)* What are you saying?

HEDDA. She's saying that we'll cease to exist.

STELLA. *(Aside.)* As if anybody ever believed her performance anyway...

HEDDA. *(Aside.)* Does she really think a catty aside at a time like this is going to save her ass?

EUGENE. *(Frantically paranoid aside.)* What are they saying?

LOMAN. Okay, look – somebody's got to decide which one of us is going to be asleep.

HEDDA. That's right! We can't just all sit here like a bunch of under-written characters stuck in a bad play and waiting for some *deus ex machina* to come out of nowhere and tell us what to do!

VOICE FROM OFFSTAGE. *Fire! Everybody out of the building!*

(They all freeze. A long pause.)

Now!

(All except **LOMAN** *stampede for the wings. The lights begin to dim, and* **LOMAN** *quickly lies down on the table. Harp music is heard, and he falls asleep. After a few seconds of half-light, the harp music is reprised, and the lights come up again.* **LOMAN** *wakes up and looks around.)*

LOMAN. Oh, my God! Where am I? I must have fallen asleep! I dreamt I was putting on a Festival of Poorly-Written Plays with a bunch of nitwits, and that everything that happens in a poorly-written play was happening to us, and then there was an offstage double murder... *(A quick aside.)* or maybe it was a double suicide... *(He returns to musing.)* and then the building was on fire, and we were all trapped in the Green Room... What a nightmare!

(He exits. As the lights dim, all the cell phones begin to ring in a last-ditch attempt to lend a vapid script existential weightiness via the use of an

obscure – but at the same time, clichéd – metaphor for the disconnect of modern theatre.)

(Blackout.)

The End

www.ingramcontent.com/pod-product-compliance
Lightning Source LLC
Chambersburg PA
CBHW051413290426
44108CB00015B/2273